Border Crossing

Border Crossing

~

Amy Schmitz

Selected as winner of the National Federation of State Poetry Societies
2017 Stevens Manuscript Competition
by Erin Belieu

NFSPS Press

This publication is the 2017 winner of the National Federation of State Poetry Societies Stevens Poetry Manuscript Competition, an annual competition with a deadline of October 15th. Complete rules and information on the purchase of past publications may be obtained by visiting NFSPS at www.nfsps.com.

NFSPS Press

Cover photograph by Igor Ovsyannykov

Author photo by Molly Condit

Cover and interior book design by Diane Kistner

Book set in Adobe Garamond text with Brazilia titling

ISBN 978-0-9909082-4-1

Copyright © 2018 Amy Schmitz
All rights reserved

No part of this work may be reproduced or transmitted in any form or by any means, electronic or mechanical, including photocopying or recording, or by any information storage or retrieval system except as may be expressly permitted by the publisher, the National Federation of State Poetry Societies.

On *Border Crossing* by Amy Schmitz:

As its name suggests, *Border Crossing* is a book that inhabits the unsteady and complex spaces between fragile and often distant landscapes. Schmitz's poems, vivid and expectation-bending, challenge the reader to interrogate the multitude of ways in which traumatic experience and place are inexorably linked, as well as the ways in which war, in particular, when it endures long enough, can become a feature of a landscape that is as expected and consistent as any tree or hill or valley.

However, the war-torn landscapes in Amy Schmitz's poems do more than just show us the humanity in the tragedy of warfare; they also allow the reader to occupy the foundational complexities of these unstable spaces. These poems expose the ways in which both people and conflict are shaped by the places that they exist in.

It has been said that there is a difference between the places we make and the places that make us. In *Border Crossing*, this distinction is broken down until the graceful, simmering violence of Nairobi's Gikomba Market is indistinguishable from a diagnosis years later in the hall of a Boston hospital. Schmitz's deftly crafted conflations of place move the reader back and forth across a multitude of physical and emotional borders to produce a kind of metamorphosis that becomes the central triumph of this book.

In these poems, because we are asked to cross so many borders, both physical and emotional, we begin to evolve or mutate, and our interactions with place shift, as do our expectations for the ways in which setting is operating in these poems. This transformation continues until eventually one is no longer able to distinguish between the fear that inhabited the war-torn spaces of the past from the hope that is directing the speaker and the reader into the unsteady peace of the present and the beckoning potential of the future. Schmitz's poems sing out with this potential in order to create an entirely new landscape that, as readers, we can't help but take great pleasure in inhabiting.

—Erin Belieu, Professor of Creative Writing and Poetry,
Florida State University

Judge's notes on the 2017 winning manuscript of the National Federation of State Poetry Societies Stevens Manuscript Competition

Contents

Borders

Border Crossing.. 11
Dakar... 12
Zephyr... 13
Gikomba Market... 14
CYP284 1967... 15
Thoughts Following a Suicide, 2011..................................... 16
Dreams During Wartime I... 17
July 4... 19
Pvt. Alvarado, Fort Benning... 20
Colony... 22
i had to get a place where... 23
Fátima.. 24
Small Disasters That Amount to No Harm (It's A Girl)........ 25
One in Five.. 26
Afterward, honestly... 27
Murmur.. 28
Where the Valley Widens and Flows Out............................. 29
Drought.. 30
train out of senegal.. 31
Dreams During Wartime II... 34

Crossings

That Was Him As A Boy... 39
Homecoming.. 41
Letter to New York... 43
Skip spring.. 44
this is your last night... 45
Ars Poetica: Scripps Mercy... 46
je vois toujours anges... 47
Chaya Leah... 52
Lorelei.. 53
How to Eat a Pomegranate.. 54
Tea... 55

the verb to go is irregular	56
Grizzly	57
The Night a Woman Died on My Street	58
Turbulence	59
Battenkill	60
Dreams During Wartime III	62
Love Your Mother	64
Daughter I am saying things to you	65
Knots, Knots	66
prayer	68
Lent	69

Borders

Border Crossing

Villages disappear. Villages may be a luxury. Soldiers don't speak
English at four in the morning. Our passports are mango meat.
A woman's youngest kid turns backwards, stares at our skin.
I'm tired enough that stars curve into graves. Soldiers inscribe
each of our names into a book thick with trains. Where am I
may be a misunderstanding. Where am I may be as irrelevant as place.
Our passports are foothills we cannot eat. Well-positioned foothills
may be a luxury. A woman's youngest wears green/yellow/red.
I'm tired enough I think his name is Jeffrey. Soldiers burn their coffee
out of chicory. Soldiers lie down on yellow grass to sleep. Where I am
may be kidding me. Where I am may be fundamentally ugly.
I'm tired enough a grave seems reasonable currency. I'm tired enough
I almost give up my seat. Jeffrey reaches out and touches me.

Dakar

Give me back my country
wound around your finger,
a golden ring that tumbles
beneath tables, twirling
in dust among stones
and coins and bones.

On the other side of the fence,
a man waits to go to Dakar.
He does not know about rain
or about overshooting the airport
in darkness, confusing its lights
for stars. It can happen.

Stars are hung on tree limbs
that swing. Their hollows
store water. Countries return,
clamp around your finger
and everything purples
at the edges. You and I could map

this heat forever. Borders do not matter.
Stars do not matter. Rain
matters. Nose first, screaming and
undeterred, it pelts the earth. It roots
and wends westward. It hurts
good, this wet and violent birth.

Zephyr

The wind tastes so soft swept across tiles
outside the old city where night falls fast
against your shirt and goats rustle

on roofs. You crack cane and the sky
opens speck by speck with stars, milky
navigators for fishermen tethered boat

to lantern to boat out at sea. One more
glass of rum and I will love you
like an animal that rips through cane

with its teeth, strips back bark as violent
as kisses and spits spent reeds against rocks,
sucking wild and sweet, so incessant a need.

Gikomba Market

Roosters are men in red who sell honeycomb and cigarettes,
      crowing louder than boomboxes. Cigar fingers molest
each black petal and knob. It's not music
      but it sounds just like music. From them, we borrow a brush to sweep
our shoes clean against barricades until they sing,
      more elegant

than expatriates in common bush boots
      who suckle water as if it were communion wafers. With
overgrown mustaches and safari vests pulled over puffed
      chests, they stalk the streets with broken
tongues. Who is saying hello? The pavement grows
      to a moat, clogged with whiskered goats and thumb-sized
nuts. These men always hunt alone,

done with wives who stumble and shimmer inside
      skin so tired it hurts, robes foreign and floral. They
are the kind of women who perch patiently on limbs, gray hooded,
      to watch us die in the late sun on the black tarmac
or in the dusty bush and then, when we're dead, peck
      at our rib cages, drilling ever closer to our still-warm hearts.
That's not the same as killing

because killing cracks their manicures. They glitter like glass
      wishing it were whole again. A bottle opens well
after midnight. When will morning come? At dawn, music turns
      off. Sun softens mud. Seconds after trucks
burst, dust rises from earth as if to shelter the greenbuls
      and bristlebills that play in concrete camouflage with no guns,
only trills of danger cut short by the crack and roar
      of incandescent anger.

CYP284 1967

Everyone is dogged in their route,
even the wild wind that sweeps in open water
and swirls into crayon curls
on children's construction
paper. Tray tables must be in the upright
and locked position. Does the man
with chains around his neck
sitting in the center seat
of the center section know
Cerberus, for all his heads,
cannot swim? Are there flames

coming from the wings? Towers are
blades of grass, green sea a shard
of polished glass and home is a gull
soaring level over surf in search
of sustenance. Can it see
our shadow immersed
in deep stone anchors? We're weighed down
by amulets, books and rocks. This is no
frog rain from an errant waterspout.
This is limbs and luggage,
seat cushions turned into flotation
devices and singed with plastic
explosives over 35-square-miles.
This is bones blown onto beaches
where one day Europeans will lie
in placid repose.

Thoughts Following a Suicide, 2011

is this how it ended
no place left to land

university boy in his bed
waiting wife in Providence

this is how it ended
bruised and boozy figures in between

he arrived behind the wheel
of a blue Italian automobile

he hovered over out-of-season
avocados in the outdoor market

he loped in late spring in loose jeans
to meet wife or boy for brunch

none of these were
how it ended

he's a palm tree buffered by
fire and wild

with each slow turn the
world gets re-blown

broken pieces paved together
into glossy city centers

where he stops to mail
the last of his love letters

Dreams During Wartime I

I.

Your footsteps behind me on dirt
roads are soft as the sound
of treetops rustling
gun shots into echoes. This bag is full
of rice. I will make dinner
when we get home.

II.

There are more katydids and kerosene
lamps than magnolias and stones.
You are not starving
me to death. My undercarriage is tough—
I will always find something
to eat.

III.

Sometimes this grave
slope seems to go on and on
toward home. No guns are at our backs.
I've forgotten we have no children
left to feed. This bag of rice
is full of holes.

IV.

Scarcity has the late ache
of pleasure. It finds me moaning
in the night under shelter.
Trees have grown used to war.
I have lied
only for you.

V.

Inland, trees are sparse. Dirt
roads go I don't know where.
Even lamps lie down
in darkness.
The sea waves
to us. The man who lives
on the corner no longer wants me.

VI.

Stones buried in dirt bite
my feet. Acacia thorns snare.
This bag of rice
is empty. We have walked so long
my bones no longer know
their ending.

VII.

Smells and stones needle
my rest. I want to rise
again to be with you. Instead I lie
raw and wet, waiting
for one sweet wave
to pull me in deep.

July 4

For my neighbor who sat in a depot underneath
the parasol she keeps open for good luck,
plucking sharp decades from her skin, kissing
them away, ready to begin again while I ran berserk
around a bonfire, ecstatic the country was 200 years old.

For her pilgrimage, her flight from landlocked
poverty to port of entry, parasol
open the whole way. Even before
income she was nicknamed, careless
currency for getting across borders.

For her birds, the ones she has tamed
and eaten and the ones she has thrown into
weather so they never come back to
wander with her over hard landscape or listen to her
repeat curses and prayers in another language.

For her again, efficient as a boy, her hair
cancer-short, her late-night bottles of spirits
broken on the sidewalk, her cultivation
of birds and their loose plumulaceous
feathers pelting the earth.

For her birth name, now unspoken, that may
have sounded like a fine 3 a.m. fog
before it burned into sun, for her core—molten
and dense—for her tongue, grasp, pace and ascent.
For her loud and beautiful anthem.

Pvt. Alvarado, Fort Benning
a found poem

You can only keep these things
    a map
    a sonar scanning class
    a hygiene bag
    a refund

You can only keep tactical use of the environment

You can only keep a nonfiction book and a maneuvering manual,
    one of which you will probably throw away

You can only keep people
    who keep trying to act like soldiers

You can only keep
    two kids who try to commit suicide

You can only keep—this is important—
    pack light

You can only keep these things three times a day

You can only keep
    the same feelings as when you left

You can only keep
    double laces
    a notebook
    a toilet paper roll with no cardboard tube

You can only keep
    darken ship
    quiet ship
    zig zag

You can only keep
    the prevention of mutual interference
    brevity codes
    a Bible

You can only keep command and control

You can only keep
      a highlighter—skinny not fat
      a one-gallon Ziplock bag
      five extra one-gallon Ziplock bags
      your wallet
      duct tape which you will make into your wallet
      your shoes which you will throw away

You can only keep
      capabilities and limitation
      voice communications

You can only keep
      dying one time

You can only keep one good thing

You can only keep this day

Colony

The catch I brought back from fishing
      was a boy lying dead on the beach
in a former slave city. He stayed dead
      all through the rest of that summer
and during the midnight flight that got me
      out of there and he kept dying
along Florida's callous coast.

      He died among overgrown mangroves.
He died among astronauts and beach bars.
      He died again in March. He stayed
dead despite the rise in temperature. He stayed dead
      on cots and in barracks. He died
among combines and grain.

      He kept dying while music played.
He stayed dead while children slept.
      He died in suburbs. He died
in planned neighborhoods. He died again in dreams. His death
      was mountain-shaped. His death had fire.
He died while we stood idle.

      He died again collecting horseshoe crab
molts. He died again watching scrub jays
      and coyotes. His death was unbalanced.
His death was big as clouds. His death had
      hurricane strength.

He stayed dead through five years of no rain.
      He died in canyons and in glacier remains.
He kept dying through every harvest.
      He kept dying in the wilderness.

He died again unarmed and moving. He died
      again with hands up and back turned. He died
face down on the ground in restraints. He died
      with different names. His death was star-shaped.

i had to get a place where

rain was nothing

colors were commonplace

women wore shoes

no one sang
of long roads
and migration

of fathers not known
even as fathers passed
on the street

so freed

i fit myself
into wrought iron tables
and basalt mosaics
on avenida da liberdade

drank the distance
to sweet coves

where fish were so eager
to be caught
they laid themselves out

on rocks

and waited

to be eviscerated

Fátima

how can I be in Boston out of gas jeans brittle with

sound of ice crunching so much snow in search of you

in search of us Sahel dust rising onto tables the myth

of location men feasting on braids of young girls I

liked to listen to your words languid and shoeless be-

cause heat is irreverence then I lost you this side of

the subaltern sea south of Bowdoin suitcases so easy

to carry I could GPS a gas station but you would not

be my salvation how do I have only $12 to my name

Small Disasters That Amount to No Harm (It's A Girl)

In winter, the car in front of me slides into snow and I stop.
The driver is a Turkish woman who says, "My brother will kill me
when he finds out." I take her to work but I do not take her seriously.

The hotel room in the Catskills has a bed shaped like a heart—crushed
red velvet. In the middle of the night, I hear fist on flesh and
weeping. I decide I'm mistaken.

Small shitty souvenirs under glass and the store clerk pats me down
convinced I've stolen a blessed virgin statuette. He lets me go without
finding the rosary tucked in my bra.

Avenue A's most persistent stalker follows after my pink skort. I bend
to tie a shoelace. He caresses the streetlamp. By the time I straighten,
he's turned on to someone new.

Grouper is perfect to order for a night glossed with promise. It comes
whole, eyes and all. I finger the soft meat, pick out the bones so
it's safe to eat.

Intimate as a husband, the knife seller shoulders open the kitchen door
and spreads what he's selling on the countertop. Knives gleam.
It's just him, them and me.

Rain, two strikes of lightning and thunder sound like someone else is in
the house. I'm finished and exposed, banged awake by the storm.

Lady is the name of the dog who nips my tit, drawing droplets of blood
and leaving a scar thin as an amulet.

One in Five

    I.

He came to me at dusk
on school tracks
lit up and vacuous
and now I can't drive by schools
in summer
without feeling the cut of his gaping fly against
my hip
then my ankle
like a mosquito
gnawing my skin.

    II.

I was standing with prison in view
from his room, my clothes
binding my chin.

    III.

I believed my windows were locked. Clothes piled for wash
kept me from seeing his footprint on the quilt my grandmother
sewed with Argentella lace.

    IV.

One too many Boston sours mixed
out of sight. One too many belts
on my wrists. Turnbuckles
caught behind the headboard.

    V.

Lakes don't hide sharks. The deck left marks.
Any kind of wave-like motion brings to mind
his face. Even sleep
has such sharp teeth.

Afterward, honestly

I could hardly put on my pants

Boots first
two legs at a time
zipper down
zipper up
belt buckle in back

        I was undone
well after the age I learned to dress
and hum

        I was spread out
beneath thin sheets easy
to see or rip through

They pulled from the inside out

Scrub the nurse said
as if I were dirty and not just human

How long, how long
gutted in the sink
a minnow
dressed as bait

Murmur

Thunder warns us awake before
dawn, storm-steel light seeps in,
licks our feet and threatens our door.

Then it begins to pour.
Arrogant mosquitoes pick and feed.
Thunder warns us awake before

mountaintops tremble—tremors
knife apart fertile milkweeds,
lick our feet and threaten our door

locks, loosely screwed into wood—more
tumble and murmur than slick click. Aggrieved
thunder warns us awake. Before

safe haven can be taken, let's perform
one last rain dance full of need:
lick my feet and threaten my door,

thick with new day. This love can transform
any storm into slippery seed.
Thunder warns us awake before,
licks our feet and threatens our door.

Where the Valley Widens and Flows Out

Sweet with the soft prayer of manure spread
in spring, your soil slopes to thistle and grows
to weeds, each fruitless seed reharvested
in hope. You are more than the blacktop road
undercut by sudden storms, more than wrecked
and rusted cars left on ragged front yards,
more than April's snowflakes that burst in wet
stars on windshields. Look—glaciers bear scars as
well: red clay valleys alive with plants, clear
meromictic lakes fed from within—such
old debris it's mistaken for sand and
stone. You are unscathed by comparison—
flooded with alluvial blossoms, your
meltwaters keep tunneling toward ocean.

Drought

I.

This is thirst hallowing us, this worship
of carbon and air, carved out of glaciers,
blown over open ocean and into
any war where men fill themselves with drink.
This is thirst, this suck of rapture. One night
before bees and scorpions are ambered,
before death petrifies in stone. We lie
unadorned. This is thirst, this avarice
for something that has not resurrected.

II.

Water has disappeared into ribbons
sultry with silt that tells stories of its
rhythm, mercy and torment. Who among
us remembers how it once moved? There was
a cove we used to swim in at sundown
seasnow falling beneath, water licking
our clefts and swells, eating the smell of red
blossoms through heat. Now water no longer
rises or comes to kiss our sticky lips.

III.

Two acacia sticks tilted at right
angles may divine water that entombed
these plains millennia ago but now
rocks hold only the eulogy of ice
and the mesa sheds moonlight. Chasms cleave
passed us bone dry; nothing alive will be
left behind. We ruin ourselves—sinners
that hope to be hidden. Let's lie still here
and decide what to do while we wither.

train out of senegal

sometimes we are the ones who invent footrests
sometimes we are the ones who use them
sometimes we are the people who sell
      tamarind through train windows
           without a notion of spreading deserts

sometimes what once was war
      becomes procedural
sometimes empires have no borders
sometimes we are the ones
      who are benevolent
sometimes we're evil
sometimes we put our feet up
      on an eastbound train
sometimes we eat all the tamarinds
      while deserts creep closer

sometimes we have interesting
      conversations with strangers
sometimes we just say
      give me

           love lyrics
              my due
                  a reason
                      a beat
                          directions home

                    give me
some money
          *

all i can do is go over old ground
all i can do is grow old over
hard ground forget i was
once a penny thrown behind a kind of tree
not grown in this country
all i can do is ground this down
      to a halt

                    a hilt
                            a point
the sharp point of hair decorations
hand-carved out of tamarind trunk
forget i once was tethered
to a cart pulling sweaty tourists
across the desert forget i was
their conveyance
all i can do is feign indifference
        shock
                sleep
                        lassitude
all i can do is back track
squat above ground
all i can do is turn myself over
wait to be found
        wait to be used
forget i was once submerged
pressed flat under ocean floor
tamarind as reef
myself as seaweed

                    *

do not place me here
all surfaces are dusty
your child's face is dusty
this tamarind is dusty
the hand reaching through the window is
sometimes mine
        exchanged
                for a footrest

                    citizenship is torpor

hello your clothes
are full of dust
and i see you're hard at work
so i'll just continue to stare
at my passport

                    citizenship is currency

you have no idea what surface
you're up against this is the sometimes
we've been ignoring
this is the night between countries
and your child's
place is precarious

>	do not silence me
>		do not flatten me
>	do not invent me
>		do not winnow me
>	do not forget me
>		do not convey me
>	do not use me

>		citizenship is complicit

it's more than 100 degrees

there are hands in the window
and the train's not stopping

Dreams During Wartime II

1944

He was on a train stuck on the tracks and he smoked
12 packs of cigarettes waiting to get home.

> He was 20,000 feet above the Tyrrhenian Sea
> wishing for one sweet twist of a bottle cap.

He was flying through a box canyon made
of yellow sandstone, listening to the wind
warning him to climb out or turn back.

> He was the train blowing through a snow bank.
> He was in a B-17 smoking a cigarette
> listening to the whistle of a bomb.

He was at home and the children around him
multiplied like fish and loaves.

1968

For a long time there was a village. Then
there was a burned village.

> She washed her father's clothes by hand
> under roof shade. Birds watched.

No good her tub of goat meat
for sale near the shack of the man
who tended banyon trees along the dirt path.
He did not want her anymore.

> No monkeys.
> Spent shells.
> Flies adorned the meat.

Jewels, gems.
For a long time, she had nothing
to remove. Then she had less than nothing.

34

2001

Children were fishing, snagged
a gull by its wing, dragged it the length
of the beach.

    They pretended it didn't matter.

Children were snatched by the swell
and bowled back to shore, spit out on the sand.

    They retreated as if the lake were enemy.

Summer was over and children went back
to school, built 3-D interpretations
of *Guernica,* used real onions for eyes,
made plaster-of-Paris horse masks,
affixed lutes, window sills and lamps
to sheet music.

    Children ran from burning buildings.

Crossings

That Was Him As A Boy

If there is a bicycle and a hill, there will be rocks
at the burial. His favorite place was a swimming plank

his father built and anchored in the river.
That was me as a college girl steaming

end-of-season corn on the family grill.
If there is music there will be a whistle,

the kind a train makes to mark its imminence
even though we were still laying

pennies on the tracks. He liked to think about single
blades of grass. He used them to imitate the songs

of birds. First there was the weekend
together. Then there was the curved path.

If there is weather there will be
an open window. *Hello bridge, hello tree limb.*

He liked to bike at 6 a.m. He had a route but
he liked to pretend he didn't know where it took him.

That was us saying goodbye
outside the family summer home, the car's

windshield wipers suddenly flicking on.
If there is night there will be wind and

if there is morning it will be witness.
That was him on a bicycle near the edge

of the river listening to a train moan. First
there was the river. Then there was skin.

That was him as a boy. That was us building
paths. That was me seeing his photograph.

Hello rope, hello wrist. He often ducked under
the overpass to rest or under the lowered arm

if the train had already passed. This is the river.
This is the rock at the burial.

Homecoming

I came home
on fire
to Virginia
where roots are not grown
deep enough for
relief bags
stamped
United States.

I came home
on a breeze
bred for hurricanes
blown
across the ocean
into Virginia's
green and spacious
plantations.

I came home
after burning
fly-ridden ribs
at dusk,
fingering honey
out of clay
pots,
sweating ants
in aid trucks.

I came home
with my hands held
to concrete,
as if I were
praying
I'd been born here.
(I had been
born here.)

I came home
to language

at least:
Welcome back
the border guard said,
as if I came home
to be received.

Letter to New York

I am writing as the last flames
of the season are being sucked
up by some Arctic wind
from the Canadian Rockies.

What I mean to say is:
Hello. How are you? Are you well?
I wonder why you don't
want me anymore. Or

I wonder why garbage trucks
don't grind up the block
nightmaring slumber. Or
there used to be

only bottles in my bedroom
and dead-of-night
blackouts, mornings sick
with orange streetlights.

I am writing still
in clothes from yesterday.
No hurricanes, no kin.
What I mean to say is: last

time I saw you it was post-funeral,
smoking cigars in the Catskills,
laugh lines starting to flower.
Remember the envelope

of mountains? I am writing
far from depressions, fingers
and gaps. What I mean is I'm
lost in ridges and deposits

wishing you nothing
but earth-shaping garnets,
green watershed,
all the kills after.

Skip spring

I couldn't sleep last night so
thought of your white sheets

in Ontario County
before we went fishing or swimming—

lake trout against our skin. Three things
brought you to mind

in a midtown room filled with
the smell of sirloin from the grill

eleven floors below: trees free
of buds on the ride from the airport

though I knew somewhere in another
state a girl was checking

poplar and larch for signs of rebirth; dark
highrise windows—empty as if

everyone lives in mortar; and a video of a ruined
shoe being resoled so

it looked new again almost. Please
tell me we really slept by the lake

and that our hair grew weedy from
water. Finally I dreamt of boys

playing street hockey at first thaw,
girls bouncing a ball on the curb, aching

to be noticed. I knew it was you
flung in the air higher than you'd hoped.

this is your last night

If I start when we were young—
    algae blossoms in the river.

Is it possible I was pressed against
    a window? Ghosts wandering around

sideways. I wonder what you talked about,
    as if breath weren't enough. Fireflies

in the garden were braver than dusk.

If I start again,
    when we were young:

algae blossomed in the river.
    Is it possible

I was pressed sideways against the window?
    Fireflies wandered in the garden, just enough.

You ghosts were braver than dusk—
    what did you talk about?

Fireflies were in the garden. What were they
    possible of? Let me start again.

We were young ghosts,
    wandering. I pressed against the window.

Algae blossomed sideways.
    Breath and dusk were enough.

Ars Poetica: Scripps Mercy

Even the building is a paradigm.
Its floors are concealed—the Ghost
of Christmas Present keeps children
beneath his robe. (Are there no
hospitals? Are there no gravestones?)
There are no miracles, only underground
parking garages and cement
passageways the dead-to-be plod.

Even the building is contorted.
How did we end up in wing
D, which did not extend from wing C?
Patterns are broken. Plumae are on
the floor, the breast lays
abnormally. Squeeze when it hurts.
The shape of your face
is the same as your mother's.

Even the building has loss.
Shedding paint on sills
is the least of it. Locks and sprockets
are missing. A woman drops
flowers in the waiting room. "For you,"
she says again and again.
When she finally leaves,
our breath resumes.

Even the building is poetic.
Oncology sits so well next
to radiology; the placement of hematology
is a little discordant. Note the rhythms,
the needle and stent, the elegant
design of liver, kidney, bladder—the body
in diagram. Try to understand
the syntax. Is this what the poet meant?

je vois toujours anges

      I.

On diagnosis day
      I went down to the dank
of our house, huddled
      by the water heater,
howled.

      We have a right to our bodies,
don't we?—
      to their musty meats, webs,
rough-cut beams.
      We have a right to their warm
waters, to their dead
      spaces, screws
and hinges.

      Ask yourself,
what is our first task
      in this new world.
Ask yourself, am I
      sated.

      II.

Sift. Sift some more.

Then make a well.

Dissolve.

      III.

One of us will reach the bottom of the casket before the other. One of us will decide which shoes and shirt, ring or no ring. One of us will pick out the wood, which lining the other will finally lay in. Until then, why not wear every day the blue silk flowered underwear bought in Paris before we married?

IV.

Will you marry me
on the couch
while the children
are at school,
while the mailman
stuffs envelopes and catalogs
through the slit
in the door?

Will you marry me
on the piano bench
while the oven timer
beeps—bread
is done, bread
is overdone, bread
is burned—
while the dog outside
the door begs
let me in?

V.

When you come
      to me again,
one of us is already
      dead. It seems
that way, doesn't it—

      our bodies lying
to us, hiding what's on top
      an ovary,
behind a uterine wall, tucked under
      the fin
of a lung. We choke
      on what we come from:
trees, sand, sea, stars, blackness, one
      exquisite burst.

In sleep, you turn. I forgive you
    for shedding me.
I forgive you for climbing
    out of me.
A gust of wind
    against the window
wakes us. Plows
    bladerun. Ice
webs. Limbs
    acquiesce.

Ask yourself, is it over
    yet.

VI.

One of us will decide brass knobs, brushed nickel handles. One of us will decide God or worms, ashes or earth. In Paris, I had no choice but to bury myself among all the small throbbing colors of the city, spare myself their prolificacy. Your spine came to me and I wanted to grate against its bricks and mortar until I was raw, until I self-destructed, until I was smoke.

VII.

Flour your surface.

Knead.

Let sit.

VIII.

Will you marry me
against the bookshelf
while machines pulse
and vibrate,
while doctors leave
unambiguous messages
in husky voices?

Will you marry me
on the hardwood floors
while the neighbors bang
car doors, while one calls
to the other "Are you
coming?" and the other cries
"Yes, I'm coming."

    IX.

Home is guts. The aftertaste
    of chemo
is yeasty.
    Bread settles. I begin
to drink.
    I begin to stockpile sympathy
dinners in the French-door freezer.
    The aftermath of chemo
is languor.
    Think of me as vapor, think of me
as an angel.

    We must go back
to the beginning,
    somewhere dark
and unfinished, made
    of pebbles and joists,
voluminous and hidden,
    made of atoms
and dust.

    Ask yourself,
what is this system
    we exist in.
Ask yourself,
    am I bitter.

X.

On rue de l'Étoile, I craved your garden, the heft and length of
you, the root and fact of you, your slow rouse, your thin touch,
your water, breath and dirt. The silt of you coated my tongue.
A woman next to me said: *avec toi, je vois toujours anges.*

XI.

Rise.

Punch down.

Form again.

XII.

On diagnosis day, I built
      an altar and prayed
to the hot water heater,
      to the screws, hinges, wire and rope
and all the small things that hold
      us together.

We can't always be
      home, waiting for storms,
wedded
      to our bodies, we can't always be
Gods. We are
      fractured
and nebulous. We are
      vagabonds.

Ask yourself, am I
      ready.
Ask yourself,
      was it worth it.

Chaya Leah

This is how we live—our pigment
breaks down. Spots on our livers, spots
on our ovaries. Always be vigilant.
Always be moving. The rabbi
at our friend's funeral plays guitar.
She was 50 and lived 46 years
without knowing what would kill her
already lived inside her. Let's
sing it out. Let's study. Greenery outside
the windows has no time left.
This is how we pray—standing,
opening hymnbooks, turning our heads
away from trees. One
season drops then another
and another. The rabbi sings a nigun.
Stay present. Stay exalted. Fall
comes in hard. This is how
we bury.

Lorelei

We were underwater—
      it felt fertile, we crawled out
of images taken by some boys
      we can't remember, went
in search of female art, stolen
      books, greedy cigarettes sucked while
coins touched our eyelids. We owned
      nothing but a collection of lost
shoes sculpted on the kitchen table
      near enough a prison, sirens
were always imminent.

There was so much more to us
      than lilies and hydrangeas—
we were seasons.
      Weather changed and we
touched fog with our fingertips,
      blazed with red
lipstick, howled for how many
      people could lose only one shoe.

How can the whole world
      now be lost? Tattoos climb
my wrist, waiting to be touched,
      old ropes less kissed
than floors I wake up on.
      Weather is relentless—
hour, hour, second: just enough
      time is left.
Your white sheets still
      drop on my skin.

How to Eat a Pomegranate

Score skin so lightly

slices can't be seen

Cut at the lip

Soft pith same color as northern
sky after snow falls
to dirt

Brush arils
into your palm

Embryonic

You are temporarily stained
red

Turn sideways

No one should see
this feast

Tea

In women-soothing rooms I drink tea taste

you herbal not medicinal no set-

ting out before dawn so your mother does-

n't find us I'm a silly painting of

a woman reading books next to lilies

or at least that's on the clinic wall such

a silent room all I mean by taste is

glasshouse flowers exist to pleasure you

the verb to go is irregular

a man I wanted to love
held his breath
passed the cemetery

this was in a different country
where bodies weren't embalmed
or well-buried

during the rainy season
I wanted him to wade
barefoot through mud
to bring me such
shiny shoes held at the waist

because no one loves
like earth that cannot be
shaken

but even the language there
stayed
unmarried

disengaged
I took myself back
to where bodies
are bathed more than
cherished

and loved another man

though I still found
crows circling overhead
reassuring

Grizzly

In the wilderness of graves I question

purgatory   even trees only stand or

lay   they are not perpetually falling

so much easier to believe in the North

American grizzly bear foraging for food

after a hibernation   what a way

to winter midlife as if there will always

be more berries   I've watched these plots

all day   I've felt the earth breaking small

bones   I've heard no moaning   mouths

are sealed for a reason and then it's time

for digging   I thought it would be like

circling above the tree tops   a way to stay

present without really staying   I am here

on your anniversary three days

late   the day of resurrection but all that's rising

is the dead scent of mown grass   the leaden feathers

of bird drift   I need a good season's

sleep to get away from this view of

polished stones   or else someone to release me

back to earth   wake me

to a new version of myself

The Night a Woman Died on My Street

I wished we were made of something different,
something unleached, like soil
layered with guano and made fertile
into another season.

Or limestone caves wet and breathing
honeycomb-carved by salt water's
slow precipitation, or salt water
deposited at the mouth of a mineral spring.

Or upwellings blown shoreward
gifting plankton to sunfish to
fishermen, or plankton
that drift lightly across oceans.

Or waves that angle
through space until, just below
the horizon line, they break
into new day.

Turbulence

One hole in the fluid flow
of air might be enough to splinter
back to earth or blow into nothing
more than mist but that's not how machines
work.
   Nearer the sun, I'm tense
as a bullet sliding into its chamber
and as useful—good only once,
then a shell. So ram me. Oil
me. I would love to go off half-
cocked. I would love to be hoisted
to your shoulder or held
against your cheek.
      Gusts barrel
by but more danger's found hair-
pinning between ice-worn rocks
in river basins. Clouds lift. Mountains
saying goodbye, you say. But that's not
how the earth works. It picks itself up
and foams. It glides in shadows and births
in dirt. It sloughs off what's no longer
needed. Goodbye to whom?
       In free fall,
these windows are futile. Abandoned
white caps below could be sharks
or ships. The ocean is worse
because it has no give. One quick
collision and I'd almost forgive you
so tell me again about lift and weight,
thrust and drag. Tell me again
how we get through this.

Battenkill

This poem will not refer to itself in the same way

as the red-winged blackbird on the riverbank will

not stop until it reaches the branches that hold its family.

Our father put a boat in the water.

Our mother stayed back at the house with people
    who did not like her.

This poem is built on the remnants of a glacier.
The red-winged blackbird appears as a warning.

Our father commandeered the boat to Dorset

where there was a rope swing over a quarry.

You communed with your hash pipe. You had stopped
    looking at things directly.

This poem is keeping its back turned.

The glacier carved through here 22,000 years ago.

Our father swam in the quarry as a boy.
Our mother stayed by herself in the downstairs bed-
    room. In general she cared but not that summer.

This poem cuts wide then treads water. It

wasn't the only thing you brought with you.

Somehow the boat floated away. Every moment

in this poem seems hazy.

The glacier mutated under its own weight left behind

rock ruined by substrate. After a while our mother
       came upstairs and boiled lobster for dinner.

This poem has no sides but water keeps threatening

to tip it over. Your presence was not reassuring.

The red-winged blackbird appears as a warning.

Dreams During Wartime III
after Amy Lowell

    I.

I swam in water I did not know.
It grew clearer
until at last I could see
by tilting my head toward coral reefs
a girl-child swimming with me
wearing only white underpants—
loose, so the swell fluttered
the hem, exposing her skin.

    II.

Across the ocean, men tested
weapons. They waded knee-deep
into water—tide sucking
their shoes—and hoisted
makeshift explosives
to their shoulders, aiming
for the horizon line.
Behind them, trees hid beyond
dunes.

    III.

We built a bonfire,
stacked dried driftwood
like bones.
Spent match fell
after spent match
to sand, tomorrow
pecked over by gulls.
"I was never a Scout—I don't know how to light a fire
naturally." But I already had a plan—
join somebody else's fire.

IV.

The men pounded their shoulders red
and shouted, "Fire, fire."
But their ammunition landed
just past the breaking waves.
It blossomed beneath surf
and funneled sand into air.
They did not stop aiming
at where ocean touched
dawn.

V.

I followed the swimming girl,
who never surfaced for breath,
to where flowering seagrass rippled
and waved in the swell. She was not near
enough for me to catch.

VI.

The men wished for chemicals
or an airplane—something with consequences
and weight.

VII.

I set out to swim 15 lengths
in one breath
with minimal strokes
just above the seagrass
but it was not possible.
Instead I watched the girl
swim in front of me, the shock
of her pale skin in the sun
under water, bones
that didn't exist yet. The sea spewed
blood and I swam on
through red water,
slowly arcing earth.

Love Your Mother

Dear daughter I would much rather see you
in red autumn slouching gently
toward Route 236 which can be walked
from Old Keene Mill to Pohick.
That is beyond my limit.

Your father and I tried
the old road from home to drugstore
to cemetery but we never made it. Pleasantries exchanged
in a stranger's car can be too much
effort as you age. I'd like to tell you
about crossing the Key Bridge
as a newlywed. We watched as the sky

grafted bits of heaven that
took off and landed. What big
dreams we had. They could not be described
over glasses of wine. They could not be
lived. They could not be revisited
so many years later on a Caribbean island
that had no bridges. In daylight
planes and stars are never mistaken.

Don't be afraid
of escaping. I would much rather see you
softer, if that's possible. I would much rather see you with your own
daughter. I wish we had walked farther. Go
brilliantly. Go sagely. Love your mother.

Daughter I am saying things to you

like sand seed storage
like always have something to sustain you, something
    of substance beneath your surface
always stay within yourself
withdraw but do not wither

I came from nothing
I was fed on nothing I decorated my hair
    with nothing so
I had to give you a pocket inside your graduation dress
I had to give you lockets nooks decades
I had to give you Dublin Paris Munich
    (you took Dakar Addis Nairobi)

Daughter I am saying things to you
like return but do not hurry
I am saying things to you like room ring restless
breach slip wood
lake border
you are turning them into ocean palisade downpour
I am saying things like mountain pine basin
you are turning them into canyon desert mesa

Daughter I am telling you
stay within yourself—there is no thirst for you
    elsewhere
there is no one you'll love like I do
go but do not linger

I came from nothing
I was bred on nothing I was wanted for nothing I looked
    for nothing so
I had to give you the wild outer edge green-gold spire needle-dry inland
    of Californian spring
thick skin to withstand loss
a spine to shed
curves for shelter

Knots, Knots

as for the cord that is the worker

followed by the cord that is the carrier

until churns of knots appear in which to

settle pots of winter-bloom—

                      or the memories

of adults bumping against doors and blood

blossoming in sinks, Emerson Lake and Palmer

on the stereo—

                      or knowing she was a witch

casting spells well into the Reagan years to control

seasons, sermons, deviations, to keep me

from growing—

                      or the blaze

in the kitchen, naked wings in a paper bag, the pretty

portrait of Jesus near the bathroom—

a veil for longer nights—

a skewer for binding—

a basket for grief—

                      they are everything save

eating salad someone just made while smoking,

save washing their blood down the drain

threads on their own

they are so good at

restraining

prayer

there's a horse in the distance

and i have to keep my eyes on it

because i don't want to end up like the old man

whose letters i found in the attic

after he was dead

said he was nothing more than a starting

gate

wind made him think

he was moving

he wasn't

not even prayer got him

to race

he bucked

against whatever came at him

couldn't turn around

get out of the way

only take others down with him

leave letters in an attic

along with a crucifix

that tasted like spit

yes i licked it

Lent

Everything in this new season is about loss,
no different than the season before.
Take, for example, last night's storm which will not feed
California's reserves. Or the hawk that swept overhead
in the park, forced to make way for the 747
banking over the mesa. Or the simple exertion of my husband
tending another grave in southwest Germany.
We talked on the phone before the storm
and he told me he'd seen for the first time
a bench that for years had been stationed
on the side of the road to the *Friedhof.*
What did you do, I asked
though I could hear it in his voice: he sat.
Everything in this new season is about ash.
I once knew the word for inviting someone to leave
permanently. I once held it carefully on my tongue,
as cold as the snow I ate as a child, the trails
I made dragging myself home,
the spirits I breathed up to stars. One drop
could end California's thirst, bring something
back to life again, affirm love. I told him to believe
in deliverance. Everything in this new season is about larder.
Such long days are still before us,
such mornings, such harvests. Such suns rise, saying
forgiveness, forgiveness.

Acknowledgements

Grateful acknowledgement to the following journals in which some of these poems originally appeared:

Poetry International, Zephyr
Kestrel, Daughter I am saying things
San Pedro River Review, Drought
Borderlands: Texas Literary Review, Lent, Dreams During Wartime II
Louisiana Review, Love Your Mother
Askew, Ars Poetica: Scripps Mercy, je vois toujours anges
Freshwater, Turbulence
Perfume River Poetry Review, Murmur
Bookwoman, The Night a Woman Died on My Street
City Works Press, Colony, That Was Him as a Boy
High Plains Literary Review, Homecoming
Sugar House Review, Dakar
Juked, One in Five
Modern Poets Magazine, How To Eat A Pomegranate
Quiddity, i had to get to a place where
Poetry City, Chaya Leah
War, Literature, and the Arts, Dreams During Wartime I, Dreams During Wartime III
Postcard Poems and Prose Magazine, Where the Valley Widens and Flows Out

Gratitude as well to places that helped make these poems possible:

George Mason University, Kripalu Center, Napa Valley Writers' Conference, San Diego Writers Ink, Santa Barbara Summer Poetry Workshop, The Syracuse Downtown Writer's Center, The University of Arizona Poetry Center, The Zen Center of Syracuse.

Thank you to early readers of these poems, especially Georgia Popoff. For their support, thank you to Mary and Ed Mehringer and Hans Peter Schmitz.

The National Federation of State Poetry Societies
Stevens Poetry Manuscript Competition

The National Federation of State Poetry Societies (NFSPS) is a nonprofit organization focused on poetry and education, which sponsors fifty annual poetry contests, the winners of which appear in the anthology *Encore*. NFSPS also sponsors the annual Stevens Poetry Manuscript Competition for the best collection of poems by a single poet. The contest winner receives a cash prize of $1,000, publication by NFSPS Press, and fifty copies of his or her prize-winning book. The annual deadline is October 15th, the decision is announced in January, and the prize-winning book is published in June. Complete submission guidelines are available from the NFSPS website at www.nfsps.com, where winning books and editions of *Encore* can be ordered.

Past Stevens Poetry Manuscript Competition Winners

2016

A Landscape for Loss, by Erin Rodoni (Rochester Hills, MI: NFSPS Press, 2017). Judge: Tony Barnstone.

2015

Midnight River, by Laura L. Hansen (Rochester Hills, MI: NFSPS Press, 2016). Judge: Bruce Dethlefsen.

2014

Beast, by Mara Adamitz Scrupe (Rochester Hills, MI: NFSPS Press, 2015). Judge: John Witte.

2013

Breaking Weather, by Betsy Hughes (Rochester Hills, MI: NFSPS Press, 2014). Judge: Glenna Holloway.

2012

Full Cry, by Lisa Ampleman (Rochester Hills, MI: NFSPS Press, 2013). Judge: Maggie Anderson.

2011

Good Reason, by Jennifer Habel (Rochester Hills, MI: NFSPS Press, 2012). Judge: Jessica Garratt.

2010

Lines from the Surgeon's Children, 1862-1865, by Rawdon Tomlinson (Rochester Hills, MI: NFSPS Press, 2011). Judge: Lola Haskins.

2009

Come In, We're Open, by Sara Ries (Rochester Hills, MI: NFSPS Press, 2010). Judge: Ralph Burns.

2008

Bear Country, by Dana Sonnenschein (Rochester Hills, MI: NFSPS Press, 2009). Judge: Carolyne Wright.

2007

Capturing the Dead, by Daniel Nathan Terry (Rochester Hills, MI: NFSPS Press, 2008). Judge: Jeff Gundy.

2006

The Meager Life and Modest Times of Pop Thorndale, by W. T. Pfefferle (Rochester Hills, MI: NFSPS Press, 2007). Judge: Patricia Fargnoli.

2005

Harvest, by Budd Powell Mahan (Rochester Hills, MI: NFSPS Press, 2006). Judge: Lawson Inada.

2004

Aqua Curves, by Karen Braucher (Rochester Hills, MI: NFSPS Press, 2005). Judge: Peter Meinke.

2003

The Zen Piano Mover, by Jeanne Wagner (Rochester Hills, MI: NFSPS Press, 2004). Judge: Ruth Berman.

2002

A Thousand Bonds: Marie Curie and the Discovery of Radium, by Eleanor Swanson (Rochester Hills, MI: NFSPS Press, 2003). Judge: Bruce Eastman.

2001

The Fine Art of Postponement, by Jane Bailey (Rochester Hills, MI: NFSPS Press, 2002). Judge: Donna Salli.

2000

The Stones for a Pillow, by Diane Glancy (Rochester Hills, MI: NFSPS Press, 2001). Judge: David Sutherland.

1999

Binoculars, by Douglas Lawder (Rochester Hills, MI: NFSPS Press, 2000). Judge: Kenneth Brewer.

1998

Singing in the Key of L, by Barbara Nightingale (Rochester Hills, MI: NFSPS Press, 1999). Judge: Sue Brannan Walker.

1997

Weighed in the Balances, by Alan Birkelbach (Austin, TX: Plainview Press, 1998). Judge: Anne Marx.

1996

Shadowless Flight, by Todd Palmer (Deerfield, IL: Lake Shore Publishing, 1997). Judge: Michael Bugeja.

1995

I Have Learned Five Things, by Elaine Christensen (Deerfield, IL: Lake Shore Publishing, 1996). Judge: Michael Dennis Browne.

1994

A Common Language, by Kathryn Clement (Deerfield, IL: Lake Shore Publishing, 1995). Judge: David Baker.